THE BIGGEST NAMES OF VIDEO GAMES

ARIE KAPLAN

Lerner Publications Company • Minneapolis

NOTE TO READERS: Not all games are appropriate for players of all ages. Remember to follow video game rating systems and the advice of a parent or guardian when deciding which games to play.

Lerner Publications Company
A division of Lerner Publishing Group, Inc.
241 First Avenue North
Minneapolis, MN 55401 U.S.A.

Website address: www.lernerbooks.com

Content Consultant: Crystle Martin, postdoctoral researcher, Digital Media and Learning Hub at the University of California, Irvine

Library of Congress Cataloging-in-Publication Data
Kaplan, Arie.
    The biggest names of video games / by Arie Kaplan.
        pages   cm. — (Shockzone—games and gamers)
    Includes index.
    ISBN 978–1–4677–1253–8 (lib. bdg. : alk. paper)
    ISBN 978–1–4677–1780–9 (eBook)
    1. Video games—Juvenile literature. 2. Video gamers—Juvenile literature. 3. Video games industry—Juvenile literature. I. Title.
    GV1469.3.K343 2014
    794.8—dc23   2013003877

Manufactured in the United States of America
1 – MG – 7/15/13

TABLE OF CONTENTS

THE NAMES BEHIND THE GAMES

You're in the middle of playing your favorite game. Maybe you're blasting aliens, jumping on colorful platforms, or throwing a touchdown pass. **Now, let's pause for a second.** Where did all these characters and games come from? Well, they definitely didn't pop into existence out of thin air. Someone had to create them.

You might know about some of the jobs these people have. There are thousands of designers, programmers, and artists behind games. But what about the specific people most responsible for creating some of your favorite video games? Do the names Shigeru Miyamoto, Will Wright, or Todd Howard ring any bells? If you want to be an expert on video games, they should. Not knowing about them would be like an expert on exploration having no idea who Christopher Columbus is.

programmers = the people who give video game consoles the instructions needed to play games

So who exactly are the amazing people who made games like *Super Mario Bros.*, *The Sims*, and *Skyrim* possible? In other words, who are the biggest names in video gaming? Read on to find out.

Award-winning game creators like Shigeru Miyamoto make games that millions of people around the world enjoy playing. Miyamoto won the 2011 Spike Video Game Award for best Wii game.

Dec. 14, 1948.

T. T. GOLDSMITH, JR., ET AL

2,455,992

CATHODE-RAY TUBE AMUSEMENT DEVICE

2 Sheets—Sheet 1

Filed Jan. 25, 1947

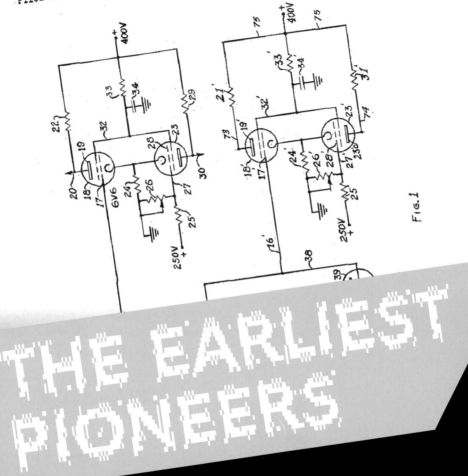

Fig.1

THE EARLIEST PIONEERS

The first wave of video game pioneers wasn't really a wave. It was more like a trickle. In the early days, very few people created games and very few people played them. These pioneers weren't making games that ordinary people could even buy. At the time, computers were crazy huge and equally expensive. The scientists who used them basically made games to amuse themselves and their scientist buddies in the lab.

It all kicked off in 1947, when physicists Thomas T. Goldsmith Jr. and Estle Ray Mann created the Cathode-Ray Tube Amusement Device. The name wasn't exactly catchy, but the machine was impressive for the time. Because the game didn't use a computer, it is not considered a true video game. Players tried to move a dot on a screen over a picture of an enemy airplane. The airplane was just a clear piece of plastic put on top of the screen, as the game was nowhere near powerful enough to actually show an airplane. Once the dot was under the airplane, the player pressed a button, and—KABOOM. Well, it was less of a "kaboom" and more of a "Oh look, the dot got a bit fuzzy."

cathode-ray tube = the device used to create the picture in old-fashioned television sets

The Cathode-Ray Tube Amusement Device was inspired by radar displays from World War II (1939–1945).

Tennis for Two was just created to entertain lab visitors, but it was the great grandparent of games like *Virtua Tennis* and *Mario Tennis*.

British computer scientist Alexander "Sandy" Douglas created the first true video game in 1952. The game, called *OXO*, was basically a tic-tac-toe game. It sounds pretty simple, but actually it was a huge breakthrough. Douglas was working at the University of Cambridge in the United Kingdom, where he was studying the way people and computers interact. In *OXO*, the computer could think for itself, and people could play against it. To be fair, the computer wasn't a genius or anything—all it could do was play tic-tac-toe. But at the time, this was a big deal.

Just a few years later, in 1958, American physicist William Higinbotham came up with a game called *Tennis for Two*. Before this, he had worked on making atomic bombs. Now his job was a bit more relaxed. Higinbotham wanted to make science more fun for visitors to his laboratory. His game showed a simple side view of a tennis court, along with a moving ball. Two players each controlled a tennis racket, knocking the ball back and forth.

atomic bombs = amazingly powerful and destructive bombs invented in 1945

Another game, *Spacewar!*, was created by Steve "Slug" Russell and his team of scientists at the Massachusetts Institute of Technology in 1961. Like *Tennis for Two*, this new game let two people play against each other. But in *Spacewar!*, they controlled spaceships and shot missiles at each other.

Douglas, Mann, Higinbotham, and Russell. Not exactly household names, right? But they deserve to be just as well known as today's top game makers. Without these early pioneers, modern video games might not exist at all.

Spacewar! was a big leap forward, but it could still only be played at computer laboratories.

RALPH BAER:
Bringing Games Home

When Ralph Baer was a young boy, there was no such thing as a video game. He was born in 1922 in Germany. Televisions were still years in the future. In 1938 Baer and his family moved to the United States. Baer's interest in electronics led him to study radio and TV technology while in college.

Ever have a good idea while you're just standing around doing nothing? Well, so did Baer. One day, while waiting for a bus, he suddenly had an idea for a game-playing device that could be plugged into a TV set. He quickly began work on the project and experimented with his TV. At first, he worked in secret. He figured his bosses at Sanders Associates, an electronics company, might react badly to such an odd project. After all, no one even knew what a video game was at that point! Finally, he couldn't keep it a secret any longer and told his company what he was up to. Surprisingly, they were fans of the idea. They gave him cash and workers, and they told him to build them a game machine.

Starting in 1966, Baer worked for two years with his team. By the end of the two years, they had made the first home video game console. Baer's bosses thought the machine could be used to train soldiers, but the electronics company Magnavox had a better idea. They bought Baer's game console and released it to the public in 1972 as the Magnavox Odyssey. It was a hit, selling more than one hundred thousand consoles in the first year alone.

Ralph Baer is more than ninety years old. He is still working, still inventing, and still an inspiration to the generations of video game creators who have come after him.

A NEW CAREER

After giving the home video game industry a jump start, Baer still had plenty of good ideas. In the late 1970s, he began creating handheld electronic toys for kids. The most famous one, *Simon*, is still around today. It was a circular toy that had four buttons, each a different color. The player would watch them light up in a random order. The player had to memorize the order and press the right button at the right time.

SHIGERU MIYAMOTO:
Super Mario's Father

A shaggy-haired, super creative, banjo-playing guy walks into your toy company in the 1970s. He says he wants to turn a gorilla and a plumber into some of the biggest video game stars of all time. Do you give him a job?

You should probably say yes—we're talking about legendary video game creator Shigeru Miyamoto. Miyamoto was always interested in art and fantasy stories. Born in 1952 near Kyoto, Japan, he originally wanted to be a comic book artist. But when Miyamoto played the 1978 video game *Space Invaders*, everything changed. He didn't want to draw comic books anymore. He wanted to make video games!

The year before that, he had started working as an artist at a Japanese toy company called Nintendo. Nintendo had started out as a maker of playing cards way back in 1889. In the 1970s, the company flirted with the idea of producing video games, but they definitely weren't known for electronic games. The 1981 flop of their game *Radar Scope* put Nintendo at risk. If the company's next game failed, Nintendo might have had to quit the video game business for good. The pressure was on for whoever made the follow-up to that game. This person ended up being Miyamoto. The game he made? *Donkey Kong.*

The game was a huge hit, but Miyamoto wasn't even close to done yet. In 1985 he created *Super Mario Bros.*, an even bigger success. By 2012 the *Super Mario* series had sold more than 200 million copies worldwide. His next game was made up of many of Miyamoto's interests. In 1986 he combined the style of Japanese comics with fantasy stories in *The Legend of Zelda*, another classic game series.

A designer could be proud of creating just one massively popular game in his or her lifetime. Miyamoto created three in the span of five years. In doing so, he became the defining game designer of the 1980s.

The Legend of Zelda: Skyward Sword, the latest title in Miyamoto's Legend of Zelda series, came out in November 2011.

YUJI NAKA: A Need for Speed

From a young age, Yuji Naka knew he wanted to get into the video game business. But at the time, no one could have guessed that a blue hedgehog with tennis shoes would be the key to his success. Naka was born in 1965 in the city of Osaka, Japan. Right after graduating from high school in 1985, he joined the game company Sega. He worked on a few games in the 1980s, but nothing that was a big success. That all changed in the early 1990s.

At the time, Sega was going through tough times. Nintendo's Mario character was selling tons of games and consoles, but Sega had no major character to compete. To fix this, the company decided to hold a competition among its employees. If anyone could think up a character who could take on Mario, Sega would create the game. Naka teamed up with a talented artist named Naoto Ohsima to design a character. They decided not to make a character who was cute or childish, but rather to create a character full of attitude. Sonic the Hedgehog was born.

The first game in the series came out in 1991 for Sega's Genesis console. In *Sonic the Hedgehog*, a blue, spiky hedgehog dashes through colorful levels. Naka wanted his game to fix some of the problems he thought *Super Mario Bros.* had. He was annoyed that the first level in *Mario* games took the same amount of time to play as all the other levels. Naka believed the game should get faster and faster as the player got better at it and advanced through the game.

Naka's obsession meant that everything in the Sonic game would be about speed. This is part of the reason Sonic is a hedgehog. Because he has spines on his back, he can just roll through enemies—he doesn't ever need to slow down. Players loved the speedy hedgehog, and the game helped Sega crush Nintendo as the sales leader in video games for 1992.

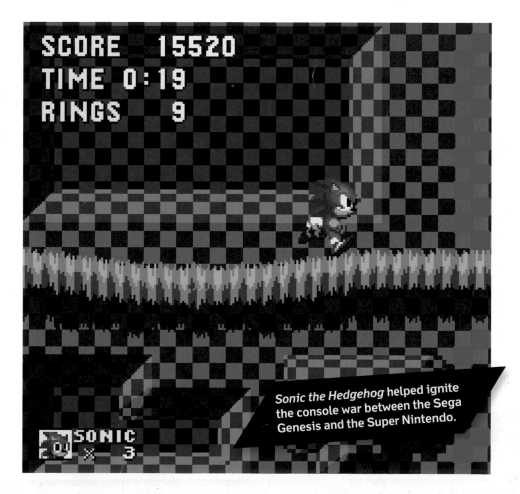

Sonic the Hedgehog helped ignite the console war between the Sega Genesis and the Super Nintendo.

It's all gone wrong there!

WARREN SPECTOR:
Imagination at Work

Ever wish you could take a class about cartoons in school? Well, just follow Warren Spector's lead. As a child, Spector was obsessed with cartoons. He loved them so much he even studied them in college. In cartoons, a story is told using moving images—just like in video games. It's no wonder Spector went on to become one of the best game designers in history.

Spector's career in games goes way back to 1983. But we're not talking about video games yet. Spector worked on pen-and-paper role-playing games (RPGs). Players sit around a table and keep track of their character using—you guessed it—pens and paper. They use their imagination to create a game world, then go on imaginary quests together.

RPGs = games where the player controls and shapes a single character, going on quests and finding items

Spector didn't jump into the world of video games until 1989 when he joined a company called Origin Systems. Once he got there, he worked on a series of RPGs known as *Ultima*. This gave him the experience he needed to create one of the best video games of all time. His legendary game *Deus Ex*, released in 2000, was one of the first RPGs where the player saw through the eyes of the main character. In a way, this combined Spector's experience with both kinds of RPGs—pen-and-paper and video games. *Deus Ex* gave players a huge number of choices to affect the story, requiring them to use their creativity and imagination to solve the game's puzzles.

Deus Ex: Human Revolution, the sequel to *Deus Ex*, was released in 2011.

SATOSHI TAJIRI: Dr. Bug

As far as nicknames go, Dr. Bug is a pretty darn weird one. But it definitely fits Satoshi Tajiri. Tajiri was born in 1965 in a quiet suburb of Tokyo, Japan. It's much more crowded nowadays, but back then his suburb was practically farm country. Young Tajiri loved to collect bugs, which earned him the nickname Dr. Bug from his classmates. He even wanted to become an entomologist when he grew up.

entomologist = a scientist who studies insects

But by the time Tajiri was in high school, his interest had shifted to video games. He took apart a video game console to see how it worked, and he started skipping school to play video games. In 1981 Tajiri even started his own video game magazine. The title might have been another fitting nickname: *Game Freak*. Eight years later, he started a video game company of the same name. It wasn't long before he realized Nintendo's Game Boy handheld console could be linked to other Game Boys through a cable. Remembering his buggy roots, Tajiri came up with an idea for a game where players could collect, trade, and battle creatures with their friends.

It took six years to create the game. Shigeru Miyamoto helped mentor Tajiri through the process of making a game. Finally, in 1996, *Pokémon* came out. Players loved linking their Game Boys together to play the game. *Pokémon* soon was turned into a cartoon, trading cards, and toys. And of course—tons of sequels.

Starting from the main character's front door, *Pokémon* let players explore and experience Tajiri's childhood hobby in a fun and exciting way.

REAL-LIFE POKÉMON

In 1999 *Time* magazine interviewed Satoshi Tajiri about how he came up with the idea for *Pokémon*. After Tajiri explained his childhood interest in bugs, the interviewer said, "So, you were collecting *Pokémon* a long time ago! Did you make the insects fight each other?" Satoshi admitted that he hadn't. But he added, "Sometimes they would eat each other."

WILL WRIGHT:
City Builder

Imagine you're the head of a big game company. You're looking for the next big hit, and a bunch of game designers come into your office to suggest ideas. One guy steps forward to present his idea. "A dollhouse for adults," he says. What would you say?

Fortunately for Will Wright (and gamers everywhere), his boss said yes, and *The Sims* was born. It would become one of the best-selling game series of all time. But we're getting ahead of ourselves here—let's rewind.

Wright was born in Atlanta, Georgia, in 1960. He studied robots and computers in college, and he decided to try video games as a career. His first big hit came in 1989 with the game *Sim City*. Players took on the role of a mayor and created their own city from scratch. Figuring out where to put homes, factories, and power lines may sound boring, but players loved making their own cities.

In 2000 Wright took the ideas from *Sim City* to the next level when he created *The Sims*. Rather than constructing a city, players would shape the daily lives of a single family. Buying furniture, choosing careers, and even deciding whether to eat junk food were all transformed from real-life activities into parts of the game. Even people who didn't normally play games fell in love with *The Sims*, proving that the video game industry had much broader appeal than once thought. Wright proved that you don't have to be a hard-core gamer to enjoy video games. And he proved that the challenges of everyday life could be just as dramatic as the challenges of a fantasy world.

Sim City first came out for computers in 1989, but it was also released on the Super Nintendo in 1991.

ROBERTA WILLIAMS:
Telling Stories with Graphics

Without graphics to back up a good story, a game would get boring pretty quickly. Originally, adventure games were entirely text-based. You had to type out what you wanted your character to do. It's hard to care about characters if you can't even see them.

"What's that? I have to type my way through an army of evil knights for the 127th time? Yawn."

So who was it that helped bring great stories and graphics to the world of games? Look no further than Roberta Williams.

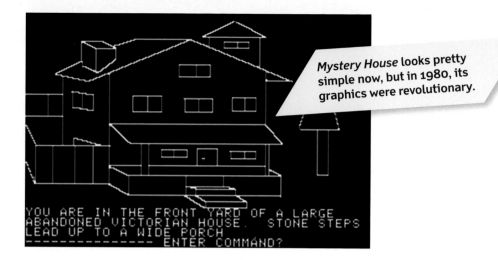

Mystery House looks pretty simple now, but in 1980, its graphics were revolutionary.

YOU ARE IN THE FRONT YARD OF A LARGE
ABANDONED VICTORIAN HOUSE. STONE STEPS
LEAD UP TO A WIDE PORCH
------------------ ENTER COMMAND?

Williams was born in 1953. She formed her first video game company in 1979, when video games barely even existed. Her 1980 game *Mystery House* was one of the first adventure games to include graphics. And the follow-up, her 1984 game *King's Quest*, took it even further. It featured colorful animated graphics that blew away the competition. Players loved the fantasy world of knights, kings, and wizards she created. It became so popular that seven sequels were made for it.

Williams retired from the video game business in 1999, but she is still remembered for changing games forever. The next time you find yourself lost in a great-looking video game world, remember that Williams was the game creator who helped make it possible.

WOMEN IN GAMING

You may have noticed that most of the names in this book belong to men. For most of the history of games, most gamers were men. Games were usually aimed at men, ignoring women. This may have led more men to get into the game business. However, that is now changing. More and more girls and women are playing video games. And following in the footsteps of Roberta Williams, more and more women are entering the video game business. There's still a long way to go before the gap between men and women is closed, but today's game creators are making it happen.

TODD HOWARD: Living in Another World

When Todd Howard was growing up in the 1980s, he was a serious gamer. In particular, he was a big fan of the *Ultima* series of RPGs. Howard loved being able to explore a fantasy world and talk to the people in it. When he played, he felt as though he was being transported to another world. He decided that if he ever got to make games as a career, this was the kind he'd like to make.

Flash forward to the 1990s. In his last year of college, Howard started playing a game called *Wayne Gretzky Hockey 3*. One day, he happened to look at the back of the game's box. The address of the company that had made the game, Bethesda Softworks, was on the box. Howard quickly realized the address was on his way home

The amazing environments of *Skyrim* encouraged players to explore every cave, crevice, and hilltop to uncover new secrets.

from school. He drove there, knocked on the door, and said "I want to make games. You should hire me." The company said no.

He asked again after graduating, but the answer was still no. So he started working at a small, nearby game company instead. But his heart was still set on Bethesda Softworks. He kept pestering them and pestering them. Finally, in 1994, they hired him. Howard has worked there ever since.

Now, let's flash forward again to 2011, when Howard's incredible game *The Elder Scrolls V: Skyrim* came out. In *Skyrim*, players can explore a huge, amazingly detailed world. You can do just about anything you could think of. One minute, you're picking wild berries in a peaceful field. The next minute, you're defending a town from a fire-breathing dragon. You can team up with some kings and wage war against others. Players love exploring the world of *Skyrim* and talking to the thousands of people living in it. Many feel as though they are transported to another world—just as Howard did when he played games as a young boy.

THE SIZE OF GAME WORLDS

The Elder Scrolls II: Daggerfall	62,394 square miles (161,600 sq. kilometers)
Just Cause 2	400 square miles (1,036 sq. km)
World of Warcraft	80 square miles (207 sq. km)
The Elder Scrolls V: Skyrim	6.7 square miles (17.3 sq. km)
Grand Theft Auto III	3 square miles (7.8 sq. km)

KEN LEVINE:
Irrational (but in a Good Way)

If William Shakespeare were alive today, would he become one of the biggest names in video gaming?

Well, Ken Levine's not far off from that. When he was growing up, he never thought he'd be making video games for a living. He was studying drama and hoping to write plays as a career.

As a student at Vassar College in the 1980s, Levine played some video games, but he didn't consider making them. After college, he wrote movie scripts and plays. Finally, in 1995, he wanted a career change. He responded to a job advertisement in a video game magazine and got into the game business.

Two years later, the company he worked for went out of business. But that didn't stop Levine. He and some of his coworkers started a new game studio, called Irrational Games. By 2007 they were ready to release their masterpiece, *BioShock*.

Like Warren Spector's *Deus Ex*, *BioShock* was an RPG in which the player saw through the eyes of the character. But *BioShock* brought a whole new level of innovation to video games. The story of the game was inspired by classic books, and players could make moral choices that would change the story. Many game reviewers considered *BioShock* one of the most artistic games of all time. Thanks to Levine and *BioShock*, many people are taking games more seriously than ever before.

innovation = new, creative ideas and features

The third game in the *BioShock* series, *BioShock Infinite*, came out in 2013.

GAME CREATORS AND THEIR INSPIRATIONS

All game creators are inspired by something. Ideas usually don't just come from nowhere. But even the ones who didn't grow up playing video games—such as Ralph Baer—had other sources of inspiration that drove them to make games. Check out this chart showing some of the things that inspired the game creators in this book—and the things they inspired themselves. If you want to make video games someday, try to think of what would go in your "Inspired By" column.

Game Creator	Known For	Inspired By	Inspired
Ralph Baer	Magnavox Odyssey	Electronics hobby	All home video game consoles
Todd Howard	*The Elder Scrolls V: Skyrim*	*Ultima*	Games with huge worlds to explore
Ken Levine	*BioShock*	Plays and literature	Artistic games with deep stories
Shigeru Miyamoto	*Super Mario Bros., The Legend of Zelda*	*Space Invaders,* comics, and fantasy stories	All game creators from the late 1980s onward

Yuji Naka	*Sonic the Hedgehog*	*Super Mario Bros.*	Fast-paced games
Warren Spector	*Ultima*	Cartoons	RPGs with player choices that affect the story line
Satoshi Tajiri	*Pokémon*	Collecting insects	Multiplayer games, character-collection games
Roberta Williams	*King's Quest*	Fantasy stories	Games with compelling stories
Will Wright	*The Sims*	Architecture and city planning	Games that take place in everyday life

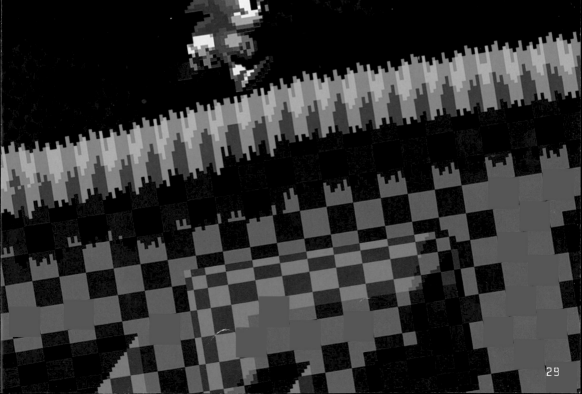

FURTHER INFORMATION

Burns, Jan. *Shigeru Miyamoto: Nintendo Game Designer*. San Diego: KidHaven Press, 2006.
Love Mario, Donkey Kong, or Zelda? Then read this book to find out more about their creator, the greatest video game maker of all time.

Edwards, Benji. *The Feminine Side of Game Design: 10 Female Game Designers*.
http://www.pcmag.com/slideshow/story/263815/the-feminine-side-of-game-design-10-female-game-designers/1
Women are changing the behind-the-scenes face of video gaming today. Take a look at this list to learn more about top female game designers from both past and present.

Firestone, Mary. *Nintendo: The Company and Its Founders*. Minneapolis: Abdo Publishing, 2011.
Shigeru Miyamoto turned Nintendo into one of the biggest gaming companies on the planet, but the company had been around for decades before video games even existed. Learn about the origins of Nintendo in this handy and interesting book.

Francis, Tom. "*The Elder Scrolls V: Skyrim*—Todd Howard Interview"
http://www.pcgamer.com/2011/10/30/the-elder-scrolls-v-skyrim-todd-howard-interview
Want to find out what happens when chickens start reporting crimes? Then read this interview. Todd Howard talks to the interviewer about some of the strange things that happened when testing *The Elder Scrolls V: Skyrim*.

Kohler, Chris. "Q&A: Shigeru Miyamoto Looks into Nintendo's Future"
http://www.wired.com/gamelife/2011/12/miyamoto-interview-transcript/
If you want to peek into the mind of a video game genius, take a look at this in-depth interview with Shigeru Miyamoto. You'll find out about Miyamoto's game-design process and learn what he thinks about the future of gaming.

Mortensen, Lori. *Satoshi Tajiri: Pokémon Creator*. San Diego: KidHaven Press, 2009.
Even if you're not a *Pokémon* fan, you might be interested in this book. Inside, you'll learn how Satoshi Tajiri overcame all the challenges of making the game.

PHOTO ACKNOWLEDGMENTS

The images in this book are used with the permission of: © iStockphoto/Thinkstock, p. 4; © Chris Pizzello/AP Images, p. 5; Thomas Goldsmith and Estle Mann, p. 6; © Fox Photos/Hulton Archive/Getty Images, p. 7; Courtesy Brookhaven National Laboratory, p. 8; Joi Ito, p. 9; © AP Images, p. 10; Evan Amos, p. 11; © Nintendo Co./AP Images, p. 13; © Lucas Jackson/AP Images, p. 12; © Kevin Winter/Getty Images, p. 14; Red Line Editorial, pp. 15, 19, 21, 23, 25, 28–29; © Jae C. Hong/AP Images, p. 16; © PRNewsFoto/ SquareEnix, Inc./AP Images, p. 17; © The Yomiuri Shimbun/AP Images, p. 18; © Marcio Jose Sanchez/AP Images, p. 20; © Mark Lennihan/AP Images, p. 22; © Mark Davis/ Getty Images, p. 24; © Mark Davis/WireImage/Getty Images, p. 26; © 2K Games/ Irrational Games/AP Images, p. 27.

Front cover: FELIX ORDONEZ/REUTERS/Newscom.

Main body text set in Calvert MT Std Regular 11/16.
Typeface provided by Monotype Typography.